Quick pocket size Revision Guide for Data Science field-Part1

Table of Contents:

This Table of Contents provides a structured approach to understanding and working with Python libraries for data science and machine learning. Each section is designed to guide you through the concepts and practical applications of the libraries, ensuring a logical flow from basic to advanced topics.

Introduction

Understanding Python libraries for data science and machine learning is crucial for effectively managing and analyzing data. Below is a detailed overview and workflow of data science projects, which will provide you with a comprehensive guide to navigate through the process.

---

1. Overview of Python Libraries for Data Science

Python offers a robust ecosystem of libraries that streamline data manipulation, analysis, and visualization. Here's a summary of the most commonly used libraries:

1.1. Pandas

- **Purpose:** Data manipulation and analysis.
- **Key Components:**
  - **Data Structures:** Series and DataFrame for handling data.
  - **Features:** Data loading, cleaning, exploration, and manipulation.

1.2. NumPy

- **Purpose:** Numerical operations and array handling.
- **Key Components:**
  - **Arrays:** ndarray for multi-dimensional data.
  - **Features:** Mathematical operations, linear algebra, and array manipulations.

1.3. Scikit-learn

- **Purpose:** Machine learning algorithms and tools.
- **Key Components:**
  - **Data Splitting:** Train-test split, cross-validation.
  - **Preprocessing:** Scaling, encoding.
  - **Model Building:** Training, tuning, and evaluating models.

1.4. Seaborn

- **Purpose:** Statistical data visualization.
- **Key Components:**
  - **Plot Types:** Histograms, scatter plots, bar plots, regression plots.
  - **Features:** High-level interface for drawing attractive statistical graphics.

1.5. Matplotlib

- **Purpose:** General-purpose plotting library.
- **Key Components:**
  - **Plot Types:** Line plots, bar plots, pie charts.
  - **Features:** Customizations for creating publication-quality plots.

1.6. Other Libraries

- **SciPy:** Advanced mathematical functions and algorithms.

- **Statsmodels:** Statistical modeling and hypothesis testing.
- **TensorFlow/PyTorch:** Deep learning frameworks for building and training neural networks.

---

2. General Workflow of Data Science Projects

A typical data science project follows a structured workflow, ensuring that all stages of the project are covered. Here's a detailed breakdown:

2.1. Problem Definition

- **Objective:** Clearly define the problem you're trying to solve or the question you want to answer.
- **Tasks:**
    - Identify business goals or research questions.
    - Determine the type of analysis required (e.g., classification, regression).

2.2. Data Collection

- **Objective:** Gather relevant data from various sources.
- **Tasks:**
    - **Source Identification:** Determine where data will come from (databases, APIs, web scraping).
    - **Data Acquisition:** Use libraries like Pandas for loading data from files (CSV, Excel), requests or beautifulsoup for web scraping.

2.3. Data Exploration

- **Objective:** Understand the data's structure and content.
- **Tasks:**
    - **Initial Inspection:** Use Pandas to check the first few rows, data types, and summary statistics.

- **Visualization:** Employ Seaborn or Matplotlib to visualize data distributions and relationships.

2.4. Data Cleaning

- **Objective:** Prepare the data for analysis by addressing inconsistencies and missing values.

- **Tasks:**

  - **Handling Missing Values:** Impute or remove missing data using Pandas.

  - **Removing Duplicates:** Identify and remove duplicate entries.

  - **Data Transformation:** Normalize or standardize data if necessary.

2.5. Feature Engineering

- **Objective:** Enhance the data to improve model performance.

- **Tasks:**

  - **Feature Selection:** Choose relevant features using statistical methods or domain knowledge.

  - **Feature Creation:** Create new features from existing data (e.g., combining date fields).

2.6. Data Preprocessing

- **Objective:** Prepare data for machine learning algorithms.

- **Tasks:**

  - **Scaling:** Standardize or normalize data using Scikit-learn's StandardScaler or MinMaxScaler.

  - **Encoding:** Convert categorical variables into numerical formats using techniques like one-hot encoding.

2.7. Model Building

- **Objective:** Develop a predictive model based on the prepared data.
- **Tasks:**
  - **Selecting Algorithms:** Choose appropriate machine learning models (e.g., regression, classification).
  - **Training Models:** Train models using Scikit-learn's various algorithms (e.g., LogisticRegression, RandomForestClassifier).

2.8. Model Evaluation

- **Objective:** Assess the model's performance.
- **Tasks:**
  - **Metrics Calculation:** Use metrics such as accuracy, precision, recall, F1-score, or ROC-AUC to evaluate the model.
  - **Cross-Validation:** Implement techniques like k-fold cross-validation to ensure the model generalizes well.

2.9. Model Tuning

- **Objective:** Improve the model's performance by optimizing hyperparameters.
- **Tasks:**
  - **Hyperparameter Tuning:** Use methods such as Grid Search or Random Search (Scikit-learn).
  - **Validation:** Test the tuned model on validation data to verify improvements.

2.10. Model Deployment

- **Objective:** Integrate the model into a production environment.
- **Tasks:**

- o **Exporting Models:** Save models using libraries like joblib or pickle.
- o **Deployment:** Implement the model into applications or services for real-time predictions.

2.11. Monitoring and Maintenance

- **Objective:** Ensure the model remains effective and relevant.
- **Tasks:**
  - o **Performance Monitoring:** Continuously monitor model performance and update it as needed.
  - o **Data Drift:** Track changes in data patterns that might affect model accuracy.

2.12. Reporting and Documentation

- **Objective:** Communicate findings and insights.
- **Tasks:**
  - o **Visualization:** Use Seaborn and Matplotlib to create visual representations of results.
  - o **Documentation:** Document the methodology, results, and decisions made throughout the project.

This comprehensive guide provides a structured approach to handling data science projects, from understanding the available Python libraries to implementing a complete workflow. Each stage is crucial for ensuring that data is effectively analyzed and insights are accurately derived.

Here's a detailed breakdown of the **Pandas** library, covering each subtopic in a structured manner:

---

2. Pandas

Pandas is a powerful library in Python used for data manipulation and analysis. It provides data structures and functions needed to work efficiently with structured data.

2.1. Introduction to Pandas
- **Overview:**

  - Pandas is built on top of NumPy and provides two primary data structures: Series and DataFrame.

  - It is essential for data wrangling, cleaning, and analysis.

- **Key Features:**

  - Easy data manipulation with intuitive APIs.

  - Handling of missing data.

  - Efficient operations on large datasets.

2.2. Data Structures
Pandas offers two main data structures: Series and DataFrame.

2.2.1. Series

- **Definition:** A one-dimensional labeled array capable of holding any data type.

- **Creating a Series:**

```python
import pandas as pd

# From a list
s = pd.Series([1, 2, 3, 4, 5])

# From a dictionary
s_dict = pd.Series({'a': 1, 'b': 2, 'c': 3})
```

- **Accessing Data:**

```python
# Access by index
print(s[0])  # Output: 1

# Access by label
print(s_dict['b'])  # Output: 2
```

- **Operations:**

```python
# Arithmetic operations
s2 = s + 10  # Adding 10 to each element
```

2.2.2. DataFrame

- **Definition:** A two-dimensional labeled data structure with columns of potentially different types.
- **Creating a DataFrame:**

```python
# From a dictionary of lists
df = pd.DataFrame({
    'A': [1, 2, 3],
    'B': [4, 5, 6]
})

# From a list of dictionaries
df2 = pd.DataFrame([
    {'A': 1, 'B': 4},
    {'A': 2, 'B': 5},
    {'A': 3, 'B': 6}
])
```

- **Accessing Data:**

```python
# Accessing columns
print(df['A'])

# Accessing rows by index
print(df.iloc[0])

# Accessing rows by label
print(df.loc[0])
```

- **Operations:**
```python
# Adding a new column
df['C'] = df['A'] + df['B']

# Aggregation
print(df.mean())
```

2.3. Data Loading

Pandas can read from various data sources to load data into DataFrames.

2.3.1. Reading CSV Files
- **Function:** `pd.read_csv()`
- **Example:**

```python
df = pd.read_csv('data.csv')
```

- **Options:**
  - `sep`: Delimiter (default is comma).
  - `header`: Row number to use as column names.

2.3.2. Reading Excel Files
- **Function:** `pd.read_excel()`
- **Example:**

```python
df = pd.read_excel('data.xlsx', sheet_name='Sheet1')
```

- **Options:**
  - `sheet_name`: Specify the sheet to read.

- `header`: Row number to use as column names.

2.3.3. Reading SQL Data
- **Function:** `pd.read_sql()`
- **Example:**

```python
import sqlite3

conn = sqlite3.connect('database.db')
df = pd.read_sql('SELECT * FROM table_name', conn)
```

- **Options:**
  - `con`: Connection object.
  - `sql`: SQL query to execute.

2.4. Data Exploration

Exploring data helps to understand its structure and summary statistics.

2.4.1. Viewing Data
- **Functions:**
  - `df.head()`: View the first few rows.
  - `df.tail()`: View the last few rows.

- `df.sample()`: View random samples.

- **Example:**
```python
print(df.head())
```

2.4.2. Summary Statistics
- **Functions:**
  - `df.describe()`: Summary statistics for numerical columns.
  - `df.info()`: General information about the DataFrame.
  - `df.value_counts()`: Count of unique values in a column.

- **Example:**
```python
print(df.describe())
```

2.5. Data Cleaning
Data cleaning involves handling missing data and removing duplicates.

2.5.1. Handling Missing Values
- **Functions:**
  - `df.dropna()`: Remove missing values.

- `df.fillna()`: Replace missing values.

- **Example:**
  ```python
  df_cleaned = df.dropna()  # Drop rows with missing values
  df_filled = df.fillna(0)  # Replace missing values with 0
  ```

2.5.2. Removing Duplicates
- **Function:** `df.drop_duplicates()`
- **Example:**

  ```python
  df_unique = df.drop_duplicates()
  ```

2.6. Data Manipulation
Manipulating data involves filtering, sorting, and grouping data.

2.6.1. Filtering Data
- **Example:**

  ```python
  filtered_df = df[df['column'] > 10]  # Filter rows where 'column' > 10
  ```

2.6.2. Sorting Data
- **Function:** `df.sort_values()`
- **Example:**

```python
sorted_df = df.sort_values(by='column', ascending=False)
```

2.6.3. Grouping Data
- **Function:** `df.groupby()`
- **Example:**

```python
grouped_df = df.groupby('column').mean()  # Group by 'column' and calculate mean
```

2.7. Data Transformation
Transforming data involves applying functions and merging datasets.

2.7.1. Applying Functions
- **Function:** `df.apply()`
- **Example:**

```python
df['new_column'] = df['column'].apply(lambda x: x * 2)  # Apply
function to a column
```

2.7.2. Merging and Joining Data
- **Functions:**
  - `pd.merge()`: Merge DataFrames.
  - `df.join()`: Join DataFrames by index.

- **Example:**
```python
df_merged = pd.merge(df1, df2, on='key')  # Merge on a common
key
```

2.8. Data Exporting
Exporting data involves saving DataFrames to various formats.

2.8.1. Writing to CSV
- **Function:** `df.to_csv()`
- **Example:**

```python
df.to_csv('output.csv', index=False) # Save DataFrame to CSV
without row indices
```

```
```

2.8.2. Writing to Excel

- **Function:** `df.to_excel()`

- **Example:**

```python
df.to_excel('output.xlsx', sheet_name='Sheet1', index=False)  # Save
DataFrame to Excel
```

This structured approach provides a clear and detailed overview of how to use the Pandas library effectively for data manipulation and analysis. Each section covers essential functionalities and common use cases, helping you to understand and apply Pandas in your data science projects

3. NumPy

NumPy (Numerical Python) is a fundamental library for scientific computing in Python. It provides support for arrays and matrices, along with a collection of mathematical functions to operate on these data structures.

3.1. Introduction to NumPy

- **Overview:**

  - NumPy is a powerful library for numerical computing.

  - It provides support for multi-dimensional arrays and matrices, along with a wide range of mathematical functions.

  - It is the foundation for many other scientific computing libraries in Python.

- **Key Features:**

- Efficient array operations.

- Mathematical functions for numerical calculations.

- Integration with other libraries like SciPy, Pandas, and Scikit-learn.

3.2. Arrays

Arrays are the core data structure in NumPy. They allow for efficient storage and manipulation of numerical data.

3.2.1. Creating Arrays

- **Using `numpy.array()`:** Create an array from a list or tuple.

```python
import numpy as np

# From a list
array_from_list = np.array([1, 2, 3, 4, 5])

# From a tuple
array_from_tuple = np.array((1, 2, 3, 4, 5))
```

- **Using `numpy.zeros()`, `numpy.ones()`, and `numpy.arange()`:** Create arrays with specific values.

```python
```

```python
# Array of zeros
zeros_array = np.zeros((3, 3))


# Array of ones
ones_array = np.ones((2, 2))


# Array with a range of values
range_array = np.arange(0, 10, 2)  # Start, Stop, Step
```


- **Using `numpy.linspace()`:** Create an array with evenly spaced values.


```python
linspace_array = np.linspace(0, 1, 5)  # Start, Stop, Number of samples
```


3.2.2. Array Operations
- **Indexing and Slicing:**


```python
# Accessing elements
element = array_from_list[2] # Access element at index 2
```

```python
# Slicing
slice_array = array_from_list[1:4]  # Elements from index 1 to 3
```

- **Reshaping Arrays:**

```python
reshaped_array = array_from_list.reshape((1, 5))  # Reshape to 1 row and 5 columns
```

- **Array Operations:**

```python
# Element-wise operations
array_sum = array_from_list + 10  # Add 10 to each element

# Matrix operations
matrix = np.array([[1, 2], [3, 4]])
transposed_matrix = matrix.T  # Transpose the matrix
```

3.3. Mathematical Functions

NumPy provides a wide range of mathematical functions for array operations.

3.3.1. Aggregation Functions

- **Functions:**

  - `np.sum()`: Sum of array elements.

  - `np.mean()`: Mean of array elements.

  - `np.max()`: Maximum value in the array.

  - `np.min()`: Minimum value in the array.

- **Examples:**

```python
array = np.array([1, 2, 3, 4, 5])

total_sum = np.sum(array)  # 15
mean_value = np.mean(array)  # 3.0
max_value = np.max(array)  # 5
min_value = np.min(array)  # 1
```

3.3.2. Element-wise Operations

- **Functions:**

  - `np.sqrt()`: Square root of each element.

  - `np.exp()`: Exponential of each element.

  - `np.log()`: Natural logarithm of each element.

- **Examples:**

```python
array = np.array([1, 4, 9, 16, 25])

sqrt_array = np.sqrt(array)  # [1., 2., 3., 4., 5.]
exp_array = np.exp(array)  # Exponential of each element
log_array = np.log(array)  # Natural logarithm of each element
```

3.4. Linear Algebra

NumPy provides functions for linear algebra operations, such as matrix multiplication and decomposition.

3.4.1. Matrix Multiplication
- **Function:** `np.dot()` and `@` operator.
- **Example:**

```python
matrix_a = np.array([[1, 2], [3, 4]])
matrix_b = np.array([[5, 6], [7, 8]])

product_matrix = np.dot(matrix_a, matrix_b)  # Matrix multiplication
# or using @ operator
```

```python
product_matrix = matrix_a @ matrix_b
```

3.4.2. Matrix Decomposition

- **Functions:**
  - `np.linalg.eig()`: Eigenvalues and eigenvectors.
  - `np.linalg.svd()`: Singular Value Decomposition.

- **Examples:**

```python
# Eigenvalues and Eigenvectors
eigenvalues, eigenvectors = np.linalg.eig(matrix_a)


# Singular Value Decomposition
U, S, Vt = np.linalg.svd(matrix_a)
```

This detailed breakdown provides an in-depth understanding of NumPy, covering its key functionalities and operations. Each section explains how to perform common tasks with NumPy, making it easier to apply these concepts in your data analysis and scientific computing projects.

4. Scikit-learn

Scikit-learn is a powerful library for machine learning in Python. It provides simple and efficient tools for data mining and data analysis, built on NumPy, SciPy, and Matplotlib.

4.1. Introduction to Scikit-learn

- **Overview:**

  - Scikit-learn provides a range of supervised and unsupervised learning algorithms.

  - It includes tools for model selection, preprocessing, and evaluation.

- **Key Features:**

  - Easy-to-use APIs for a wide range of machine learning tasks.

  - Integration with other scientific libraries like NumPy and Pandas.

- Support for various machine learning algorithms and model evaluation metrics.

4.2. Data Splitting

Proper data splitting is crucial to build and evaluate machine learning models effectively.

4.2.1. Train-Test Split

- **Function:** `train_test_split()`

- **Purpose:** Split data into training and testing sets to evaluate model performance.

- **Example:**

```python
from sklearn.model_selection import train_test_split

# Sample data
X = [[1, 2], [3, 4], [5, 6], [7, 8]]
y = [0, 1, 0, 1]

# Split the data
X_train, X_test, y_train, y_test = train_test_split(X, y, test_size=0.3, random_state=42)
```

- **Options:**

  - `test_size`: Proportion of the data to be used for testing.

  - `random_state`: Seed for random number generator to ensure reproducibility.

4.2.2. Cross-Validation

- **Function:** `cross_val_score()`

- **Purpose:** Evaluate model performance by splitting the data into multiple folds and training on different subsets.

- **Example:**

```python
from sklearn.model_selection import cross_val_score
from sklearn.ensemble import RandomForestClassifier

model = RandomForestClassifier()
scores = cross_val_score(model, X, y, cv=5)  # 5-fold cross-validation
```

- **Options:**

  - `cv`: Number of folds for cross-validation.

  - `scoring`: Metric to evaluate model performance (e.g., 'accuracy').

4.3. Preprocessing

Preprocessing is essential to prepare raw data for machine learning models.

4.3.1. Scaling Features

- **Function:** `StandardScaler` or `MinMaxScaler`

- **Purpose:** Normalize or standardize feature values to improve model performance.

- **Example:**

```python
from sklearn.preprocessing import StandardScaler

scaler = StandardScaler()
X_scaled = scaler.fit_transform(X)  # Standardize features
```

- **Options:**

  - `StandardScaler`: Standardizes features by removing the mean and scaling to unit variance.

  - `MinMaxScaler`: Scales features to a specified range (default is [0, 1]).

4.3.2. Encoding Categorical Variables

- **Function:** `OneHotEncoder` or `LabelEncoder`

- **Purpose:** Convert categorical variables into numerical format for machine learning models.

- **Example:**

```python
from sklearn.preprocessing import OneHotEncoder

encoder = OneHotEncoder()
X_encoded = encoder.fit_transform(X_categorical).toarray()  # One-hot encode categorical features
```

- **Options:**

  - `OneHotEncoder`: Converts categorical variables into a one-hot numeric array.

  - `LabelEncoder`: Encodes categorical labels as integers.

4.4. Model Building

Building a model involves training it with data and optimizing its parameters.

4.4.1. Training Models

- **Function:** `fit()`

- **Purpose:** Train a model using training data.

- **Example:**

```python
from sklearn.linear_model import LogisticRegression

model = LogisticRegression()
model.fit(X_train, y_train)  # Train the model
```

- **Options:**
  - Different algorithms can be used depending on the problem (e.g., `LogisticRegression`, `RandomForestClassifier`).

4.4.2. Hyperparameter Tuning
- **Function:** `GridSearchCV` or `RandomizedSearchCV`
- **Purpose:** Find the best hyperparameters for the model by performing a search over specified parameter values.

- **Example:**

```python
from sklearn.model_selection import GridSearchCV

param_grid = {'C': [0.1, 1, 10], 'solver': ['liblinear']}
grid_search = GridSearchCV(LogisticRegression(), param_grid, cv=5)
```

```
grid_search.fit(X_train, y_train)
```

- **Options:**
  - `param_grid`: Dictionary with parameters to search.
  - `cv`: Number of folds for cross-validation.

4.5. Model Evaluation

Evaluating the model's performance is critical to understand how well it performs.

4.5.1. Accuracy

- **Function:** `accuracy_score()`
- **Purpose:** Measure the proportion of correctly predicted instances.

- **Example:**

```python
from sklearn.metrics import accuracy_score

y_pred = model.predict(X_test)
accuracy = accuracy_score(y_test, y_pred)  # Calculate accuracy
```

4.5.2. Precision and Recall

- **Functions:** `precision_score()`, `recall_score()`

- **Purpose:** Measure the model's performance in classification problems, focusing on precision and recall.

- **Examples:**

```python
from sklearn.metrics import precision_score, recall_score

precision = precision_score(y_test, y_pred)
recall = recall_score(y_test, y_pred)
```

4.5.3. Confusion Matrix

- **Function:** `confusion_matrix()`

- **Purpose:** Show the number of true positives, false positives, true negatives, and false negatives.

- **Example:**

```python
from sklearn.metrics import confusion_matrix

cm = confusion_matrix(y_test, y_pred)
```

```
```

- **Options:**

  - Confusion matrix helps in understanding the model's performance in more detail.

4.6. Model Selection

Choosing the best model involves comparing different models and evaluating feature importance.

4.6.1. Model Comparison

- **Function:** Compare different models based on their performance metrics.

- **Example:**

```python
from sklearn.ensemble import RandomForestClassifier
from sklearn.svm import SVC
from sklearn.metrics import accuracy_score

models = [RandomForestClassifier(), SVC()]
for model in models:
    model.fit(X_train, y_train)
    y_pred = model.predict(X_test)
```

```python
    print(f"{model.__class__.__name__} Accuracy:
{accuracy_score(y_test, y_pred)}")
```

4.6.2. Feature Importance

- **Function:** `feature_importances_`

- **Purpose:** Evaluate the importance of different features in the model.

- **Example:**

```python
model = RandomForestClassifier()
model.fit(X_train, y_train)
importances = model.feature_importances_

# Display feature importance
print(importances)
```

- **Options:**

  - Use `feature_importances_` attribute for models like Random Forest to understand which features are most influential.

This detailed breakdown provides a structured overview of Scikit-learn, covering essential functionalities and procedures. Each section helps you understand how to utilize Scikit-learn for building, evaluating, and optimizing machine learning models.

Here's a detailed breakdown of the **Seaborn** library, covering each subtopic in a structured manner:

---

5. Seaborn

Seaborn is a Python visualization library based on Matplotlib that provides a high-level interface for drawing attractive and informative statistical graphics. It integrates closely with Pandas data structures and provides functions to easily generate various types of plots.

5.1. Introduction to Seaborn
- **Overview:**

- Seaborn provides a higher-level interface to Matplotlib, making it easier to create complex visualizations with less code.

  - It is designed for statistical data visualization and comes with built-in themes and color palettes.

- **Key Features:**

  - Beautiful default styles and color palettes.

  - Integration with Pandas DataFrames.

  - Simple functions for creating complex visualizations.

5.2. Basic Plot Types

Seaborn offers a variety of basic plot types to visualize different aspects of your data.

5.2.1. Histograms

- **Function:** `sns.histplot()`

- **Purpose:** Display the distribution of a single continuous variable.

- **Example:**

```python
import seaborn as sns
import matplotlib.pyplot as plt

# Sample data
```

```python
data = [1, 2, 2, 3, 4, 4, 4, 5, 6, 6, 7]

# Create a histogram
sns.histplot(data, bins=10, kde=False)

# Show plot
plt.show()
```

- **Options:**
  - `bins`: Number of bins in the histogram.
  - `kde`: Whether to plot a Kernel Density Estimate (KDE) alongside the histogram.

5.2.2. Scatter Plots
- **Function:** `sns.scatterplot()`
- **Purpose:** Visualize the relationship between two continuous variables.

- **Example:**

```python
import seaborn as sns
import matplotlib.pyplot as plt
```

```python
# Sample data
x = [1, 2, 3, 4, 5]
y = [5, 4, 3, 2, 1]

# Create a scatter plot
sns.scatterplot(x=x, y=y)

# Show plot
plt.show()
```

- **Options:**
  - `hue`: Variable to color the points.
  - `style`: Variable to style the points.

5.2.3. Bar Plots
- **Function:** `sns.barplot()`
- **Purpose:** Show the relationship between a categorical variable and a continuous variable.

- **Example:**

```python
import seaborn as sns
import matplotlib.pyplot as plt
```

```python
# Sample data
data = {'Category': ['A', 'B', 'C'], 'Value': [10, 20, 15]}

# Create a bar plot
sns.barplot(x='Category', y='Value', data=data)

# Show plot
plt.show()
```

- **Options:**
  - `hue`: Variable to color the bars.
  - `ci`: Confidence interval for the plot.

5.3. Statistical Plots

Seaborn provides statistical plots that can help in understanding the data relationships and distributions.

5.3.1. Regression Plots

- **Function:** `sns.regplot()`

- **Purpose:** Fit and visualize a linear regression model on a scatter plot.

- **Example:**

```python
import seaborn as sns
import matplotlib.pyplot as plt

# Sample data
x = [1, 2, 3, 4, 5]
y = [1, 2, 1.5, 3.5, 2.5]

# Create a regression plot
sns.regplot(x=x, y=y)

# Show plot
plt.show()
```

- **Options:**
  - `order`: Order of the polynomial for the regression line.
  - `ci`: Confidence interval for the regression line.

5.3.2. Pair Plots

- **Function:** `sns.pairplot()`
- **Purpose:** Create a matrix of scatter plots for all pairs of variables in a DataFrame.

- **Example:**

```python
import seaborn as sns
import pandas as pd

# Sample data
df = pd.DataFrame({
    'A': [1, 2, 3, 4, 5],
    'B': [5, 4, 3, 2, 1],
    'C': [2, 3, 4, 5, 6]
})

# Create a pair plot
sns.pairplot(df)

# Show plot
plt.show()
```

- **Options:**
  - `hue`: Variable to color the points.
  - `diag_kind`: Kind of plot to use on the diagonal (e.g., 'hist', 'kde').

5.4. Customizing Plots

Customizing plots enhances readability and helps in better communication of the data insights.

5.4.1. Adding Titles and Labels

- **Functions:**

  - `plt.title()`

  - `plt.xlabel()`

  - `plt.ylabel()`

- **Example:**

```python
import seaborn as sns
import matplotlib.pyplot as plt

# Sample data
x = [1, 2, 3, 4, 5]
y = [5, 4, 3, 2, 1]

# Create a scatter plot
sns.scatterplot(x=x, y=y)

# Add title and labels
plt.title('Scatter Plot Example')
plt.xlabel('X Axis')
```

```
plt.ylabel('Y Axis')

# Show plot
plt.show()
```

- **Options:**
  - Customize the title, axis labels, and font sizes.

5.4.2. Adjusting Colors and Styles
- **Functions:**
  - `sns.set_style()`
  - `sns.set_palette()`

- **Example:**

```python
import seaborn as sns
import matplotlib.pyplot as plt

# Set the style and color palette
sns.set_style('whitegrid')
sns.set_palette('pastel')

# Sample data
```

```
x = [1, 2, 3, 4, 5]
y = [5, 4, 3, 2, 1]

# Create a scatter plot
sns.scatterplot(x=x, y=y)

# Show plot
plt.show()
```

- **Options:**
  - `set_style()`: Set the background style (e.g., 'darkgrid', 'whitegrid').
  - `set_palette()`: Set the color palette for the plot.

This structured breakdown of Seaborn covers its essential functionalities and customization options, making it easier to create and refine visualizations for your data analysis tasks.

Here's a detailed breakdown of **Matplotlib**, covering each subtopic in a structured manner:

---

6. Matplotlib

Matplotlib is a comprehensive library for creating static, animated, and interactive visualizations in Python. It is highly customizable and integrates well with other libraries like NumPy and Pandas.

6.1. Introduction to Matplotlib

- **Overview:**

  - Matplotlib is one of the most widely used libraries for plotting in Python.

  - It provides a variety of functions for creating a range of static, animated, and interactive plots.

  - It is the foundation for many other visualization libraries, including Seaborn.

- **Key Features:**

  - Extensive customization options for plots.

  - Support for various plot types, including line, bar, and pie charts.

  - Integration with NumPy and Pandas for data manipulation.

6.2. Basic Plot Types

Matplotlib supports several basic plot types for visualizing different aspects of your data.

6.2.1. Line Plots

- **Function:** `plt.plot()`

- **Purpose:** Display data points connected by straight lines.

- **Example:**

```python
import matplotlib.pyplot as plt

# Sample data
x = [1, 2, 3, 4, 5]
y = [2, 3, 5, 7, 11]

# Create a line plot
plt.plot(x, y, marker='o')

# Add title and labels
plt.title('Line Plot Example')
plt.xlabel('X Axis')
plt.ylabel('Y Axis')

# Show plot
plt.show()
```

- **Options:**
  - `marker`: Style of the marker at data points.
  - `linestyle`: Style of the line (e.g., '-', '--').

6.2.2. Bar Plots

- **Function:** `plt.bar()`

- **Purpose:** Show the relationship between categorical data and numerical values.

- **Example:**

```python
import matplotlib.pyplot as plt

# Sample data
categories = ['A', 'B', 'C']
values = [10, 20, 15]

# Create a bar plot
plt.bar(categories, values, color='skyblue')

# Add title and labels
plt.title('Bar Plot Example')
plt.xlabel('Category')
plt.ylabel('Value')

# Show plot
plt.show()
```

```
```

- **Options:**
  - `color`: Color of the bars.
  - `width`: Width of the bars.

6.2.3. Pie Charts
- **Function:** `plt.pie()`
- **Purpose:** Display proportions of a whole as slices of a pie.

- **Example:**

```python
import matplotlib.pyplot as plt

# Sample data
labels = ['A', 'B', 'C']
sizes = [30, 45, 25]

# Create a pie chart
plt.pie(sizes, labels=labels, autopct='%1.1f%%', startangle=140)

# Add title
plt.title('Pie Chart Example')
```

```python
# Show plot
plt.show()
```

- **Options:**
  - `autopct`: Format for displaying percentages.
  - `startangle`: Starting angle for the pie chart.

6.3. Customizing Plots

Customizing plots helps in making them more informative and aesthetically pleasing.

6.3.1. Adding Annotations
- **Function:** `plt.annotate()`
- **Purpose:** Add text annotations to specific points on the plot.

- **Example:**

```python
import matplotlib.pyplot as plt

# Sample data
x = [1, 2, 3, 4, 5]
y = [2, 3, 5, 7, 11]
```

```python
# Create a line plot
plt.plot(x, y, marker='o')

# Add annotation
plt.annotate('Max Point', xy=(5, 11), xytext=(3, 12),
            arrowprops=dict(facecolor='black', shrink=0.05))

# Add title and labels
plt.title('Line Plot with Annotation')
plt.xlabel('X Axis')
plt.ylabel('Y Axis')

# Show plot
plt.show()
```

- **Options:**
  - `xy`: Point to annotate.
  - `xytext`: Location of the annotation text.

6.3.2. Modifying Axes
- **Functions:**
  - `plt.xlim()`
  - `plt.ylim()`
  - `plt.xlabel()`

- `plt.ylabel()`
- `plt.title()`

- **Examples:**

```python
import matplotlib.pyplot as plt

# Sample data
x = [1, 2, 3, 4, 5]
y = [2, 3, 5, 7, 11]

# Create a line plot
plt.plot(x, y, marker='o')

# Customize axes
plt.xlim(0, 6)
plt.ylim(0, 12)
plt.xlabel('X Axis Label')
plt.ylabel('Y Axis Label')
plt.title('Customized Axes Example')

# Show plot
plt.show()
```

- **Options:**

  - `xlim` and `ylim`: Set limits for the x and y axes.

  - `xlabel` and `ylabel`: Label the x and y axes.

6.4. Saving and Showing Plots

Saving and displaying plots are essential for sharing and reviewing visualizations.

6.4.1. Saving as Files

- **Function:** `plt.savefig()`

- **Purpose:** Save the plot to a file in various formats (e.g., PNG, PDF).

- **Example:**

```python
import matplotlib.pyplot as plt

# Sample data
x = [1, 2, 3, 4, 5]
y = [2, 3, 5, 7, 11]

# Create a line plot
plt.plot(x, y, marker='o')
```

```
# Save plot to a file
plt.savefig('plot.png')

# Optionally show plot
plt.show()
```

- **Options:**
  - `format`: File format (e.g., 'png', 'pdf').
  - `dpi`: Resolution of the saved file.

6.4.2. Displaying in Interactive Environments
- **Functions:** `plt.show()`
- **Purpose:** Display the plot in interactive environments like Jupyter notebooks.

- **Example:**

```python
import matplotlib.pyplot as plt

# Sample data
x = [1, 2, 3, 4, 5]
y = [2, 3, 5, 7, 11]
```

```
# Create a line plot
plt.plot(x, y, marker='o')


# Show plot
plt.show()
```

- **Options:**

  - In Jupyter notebooks, use `%matplotlib inline` for inline display.

This breakdown provides a comprehensive overview of Matplotlib, detailing its essential functionalities and customization options. It helps in understanding how to create, modify, and save various types of plots, making it easier to visualize and communicate your data effectively.\

7. Logical Flow and Understanding Code

Understanding and working with code, especially in the context of data science and machine learning, involves comprehending how different libraries work together and how to effectively interpret and manipulate code snippets. Here's a structured approach to understanding and working with Python code:

7.1. Understanding the Purpose of Libraries

Each Python library serves a specific purpose and is designed to simplify certain tasks. Understanding the purpose of each library helps in leveraging their functionalities effectively.

- **Pandas:** Primarily used for data manipulation and analysis. It provides data structures like Series and DataFrame for handling data.

- **NumPy:** Provides support for large, multi-dimensional arrays and matrices, along with a collection of mathematical functions to operate on these arrays.

- **Scikit-learn:** Used for machine learning. It provides tools for model building, training, evaluation, and preprocessing.

- **Seaborn:** Built on Matplotlib, it provides a high-level interface for creating attractive and informative statistical graphics.

- **Matplotlib:** A versatile library for creating static, animated, and interactive visualizations in Python.

7.2. Breaking Down Code

To understand and debug code, breaking it down into smaller parts helps in grasping its overall logic and flow.

7.2.1. Identifying Inputs and Outputs

- **Inputs:** Data or parameters that are fed into a function or model.

- **Outputs:** Results or predictions produced by the function or model.

- **Example:**

```python
import pandas as pd
```

```python
# Input: File path of CSV data
file_path = 'data.csv'

# Operation: Reading CSV file into a DataFrame
df = pd.read_csv(file_path)

# Output: DataFrame containing data from the CSV file
print(df.head())
```

- **Explanation:**
  - **Input:** `'data.csv'`
  - **Operation:** `pd.read_csv(file_path)`
  - **Output:** The first few rows of the DataFrame `df`

7.2.2. Step-by-Step Execution
Understanding the code execution involves following the sequence of operations and analyzing their impact.

- **Example:**
```python
import numpy as np
import matplotlib.pyplot as plt
```

```
# Step 1: Create an array of values
x = np.linspace(0, 10, 100)

# Step 2: Compute the square of each value
y = np.power(x, 2)

# Step 3: Create a plot of x vs. y
plt.plot(x, y)
plt.title('Square Function')
plt.xlabel('x')
plt.ylabel('x^2')

# Step 4: Show the plot
plt.show()
```

- **Explanation:**
  - **Step 1:** Generates 100 values between 0 and 10.
  - **Step 2:** Computes the square of each value.
  - **Step 3:** Plots the results.
  - **Step 4:** Displays the plot.

7.3. Interaction Between Libraries

Libraries often interact with each other to perform complex tasks. Understanding how they interact helps in leveraging their combined capabilities.

7.3.1. Pandas and NumPy

- **Interaction:** Pandas DataFrames and Series are built on top of NumPy arrays. Pandas operations often use NumPy functions for numerical computations.

- **Example:**

```python
import pandas as pd
import numpy as np

# Create a DataFrame
df = pd.DataFrame({
    'A': np.random.rand(5),
    'B': np.random.rand(5)
})

# Use a NumPy function on DataFrame
df['C'] = np.log(df['A'])
```

- **Explanation:**
  - DataFrame `df` contains random numbers in columns `A` and `B`.

- The `np.log()` function computes the logarithm of column `A`.

7.3.2. Scikit-learn and Pandas/NumPy

- **Interaction:** Scikit-learn relies on Pandas for data manipulation and NumPy for numerical computations. Scikit-learn models often accept Pandas DataFrames or NumPy arrays as input.

- **Example:**
```python
import pandas as pd
from sklearn.model_selection import train_test_split
from sklearn.linear_model import LinearRegression
from sklearn.metrics import mean_squared_error

# Sample DataFrame
df = pd.DataFrame({
    'X': [1, 2, 3, 4, 5],
    'y': [2, 3, 5, 7, 11]
})

# Split data into training and testing sets
X_train, X_test, y_train, y_test = train_test_split(df[['X']], df['y'], test_size=0.2)

# Train a model
model = LinearRegression()
```

```
model.fit(X_train, y_train)

# Make predictions
y_pred = model.predict(X_test)

# Evaluate the model
mse = mean_squared_error(y_test, y_pred)
```

- **Explanation:**

  - **Data Preparation:** Uses Pandas DataFrame for input data.

  - **Model Training and Evaluation:** Scikit-learn functions are used to train the model and evaluate performance.

7.3.3. Seaborn and Matplotlib

- **Interaction:** Seaborn is built on top of Matplotlib and uses its underlying functions for rendering plots. Seaborn simplifies complex plotting tasks and can be customized using Matplotlib functions.

- **Example:**

```python
import seaborn as sns
import matplotlib.pyplot as plt

# Sample DataFrame
df = sns.load_dataset('iris')
```

```python
# Create a pair plot with Seaborn
sns.pairplot(df, hue='species')

# Customize using Matplotlib
plt.suptitle('Pair Plot of Iris Dataset', y=1.02)
plt.show()
```

- **Explanation:**
  - **Seaborn:** Creates a pair plot for the Iris dataset.
  - **Matplotlib:** Customizes the plot title and adjusts layout.

7.4. Hands-On Practice

Practical experience is crucial for understanding how to apply and adapt code to different scenarios.

7.4.1. Experimenting with Code Snippets

- **Activity:** Try modifying existing code snippets to understand their behavior and output. This can involve changing parameters, adding new features, or integrating additional libraries.

- **Example:**
  ```python
  import matplotlib.pyplot as plt
  import numpy as np
  ```

```
# Original code
x = np.linspace(0, 10, 100)
y = np.sin(x)
plt.plot(x, y)
plt.show()


# Experiment: Change to cosine function
y = np.cos(x)
plt.plot(x, y)
plt.show()
```

- **Explanation:**

  - Modify the function from sine to cosine and observe how the plot changes.

7.4.2. Modifying Examples

- **Activity:** Take example codes from documentation or tutorials and modify them to suit your own data or objectives. This helps in understanding how different components work together.

- **Example:**
  ```python
  import seaborn as sns
  import pandas as pd
  ```

```python
# Load a different dataset
df = pd.read_csv('another_dataset.csv')

# Create a histogram of a specific column
sns.histplot(df['column_name'])

# Show the plot
plt.show()
```

- **Explanation:**

  - Load a new dataset and visualize a specific column with a histogram.

This structured approach to understanding and working with Python code, especially in the context of data science and machine learning, provides a clear path for comprehending and effectively utilizing different libraries and code snippets.

8. Conclusion

The conclusion of any technical guide or tutorial is essential for summarizing the key takeaways, providing guidance on future learning paths, and recommending additional resources for continued growth. Here's how to structure this section:

8.1. Summary of Key Concepts

In this section, we recap the core topics covered throughout the guide, ensuring that the reader has a clear understanding of the main points.

- **Python Libraries Overview:**

  - **Pandas:** Data manipulation and analysis using DataFrames and Series.

  - **NumPy:** Numerical computations with arrays and mathematical functions.

  - **Scikit-learn:** Machine learning tools for model building, training, and evaluation.

- **Seaborn:** Statistical data visualization built on Matplotlib.

- **Matplotlib:** Versatile plotting library for creating static, animated, and interactive visualizations.

- **Logical Flow in Code:**

  - **Purpose of Libraries:** Each library serves a unique purpose and integrates with others to perform complex tasks.

  - **Breaking Down Code:** Understand inputs, outputs, and step-by-step execution to effectively read and debug code.

  - **Library Interactions:** How libraries like Pandas, NumPy, Scikit-learn, Seaborn, and Matplotlib work together to facilitate data science tasks.

- **Practical Application:**

  - **Hands-On Practice:** Experimenting with code snippets and modifying examples to grasp practical usage.

8.2. Future Learning Paths

This section provides guidance on how to advance from the foundational knowledge covered in the guide.

- **Advanced Topics:**

  - **Machine Learning:** Explore advanced algorithms, model optimization, and deployment techniques.

  - **Deep Learning:** Study neural networks, including CNNs, RNNs, and GANs.

- **Natural Language Processing (NLP):** Learn about text analysis, sentiment analysis, and language models.

  - **Computer Vision:** Understand image processing, object detection, and image classification.

- **Specializations:**

  - **Big Data Analytics:** Dive into tools and technologies for handling large datasets (e.g., Spark, Hadoop).

  - **Data Engineering:** Focus on data pipelines, ETL processes, and data architecture.

  - **Data Visualization:** Master advanced visualization tools and techniques (e.g., Plotly, D3.js).

- **Certifications and Courses:**

  - Consider pursuing certifications in data science, machine learning, or specific technologies (e.g., TensorFlow, PyTorch).

8.3. Additional Resources

This section lists resources for continued learning and exploration in the field.

- **Books:**

  - **"Python for Data Analysis" by Wes McKinney:** In-depth guide on data manipulation with Pandas.

  - **"Deep Learning with Python" by François Chollet:** Comprehensive introduction to deep learning using Keras and TensorFlow.

- **"Hands-On Machine Learning with Scikit-Learn, Keras, and TensorFlow" by Aurélien Géron:** Practical guide to machine learning and deep learning.

- **Online Courses:**

  - **Coursera:** Courses on data science, machine learning, and deep learning (e.g., Andrew Ng's Machine Learning course).

  - **edX:** Offers professional certifications and micro-degrees in data science and AI.

  - **Udacity:** Nanodegrees in Data Science, Machine Learning, and AI.

- **Websites and Blogs:**

  - **Kaggle:** Platform for data science competitions and datasets. Also provides courses and tutorials.

  - **Towards Data Science:** Blog featuring articles on data science, machine learning, and AI.

  - **DataCamp:** Online learning platform with interactive courses in data science and analytics.

- **Communities and Forums:**

  - **Stack Overflow:** Q&A platform for coding and technical issues.

  - **Reddit:** Subreddits like r/datascience, r/MachineLearning, and r/learnpython.

  - **GitHub:** Explore repositories and projects related to data science and machine learning.

This structured conclusion provides a clear summary of what has been covered, offers pathways for further learning, and points to valuable resources for continued education and growth in the field.

To be continued…part2